Bygone LEITH

by
Guthrie Hutton

A coaster heads away from Leith through the anarchic clutter of barges, lighters and big ships that characterised the busy port in the 1920s.

First published in the United Kingdom, 2004,
reprinted 2010
by Stenlake Publishing Ltd.
01290 551122
www.stenlake.co.uk

ISBN 978 1 84033 324 4

Below: Camera-shake has obscured the old close name in this photograph, but the street sign is of a style used in Leith and the picture was found with other (equally fuzzy) images of the docks and Newhaven. While the blurring may have made identification difficult, it has not diminished the picture's social history value: there is nothing staged about these beshawled women and barefoot children. This is an image of real lives and real poverty, and is in marked contrast to the romanticised version on the facing page.

ACKNOWLEDGEMENTS

This is the second time I have delved into Leith's story for a book of this kind. The first was in 1995 and it is remarkable how much, and how little, Leith has changed in that time. As then I have taken the old burgh boundary as the limit for the spread of the book. It's a large area, but my task of combing the streets in pursuit of detail was made easy by a splendid bus service that picked me up and put me down at key locations all over the place. I must therefore thank the transport planners and bus drivers of Edinburgh who did me proud, and all for a couple of pounds a day – great! I must also thank the many librarians who dug out obscure items, mainly in the Edinburgh Room of the City Library, but also in that splendid institution in that other city, the Mitchell Library, Glasgow. Lastly I would like to thank the people of Leith who have filled in the gaps, and in particular my wife whose childhood memories made my task easier.

FURTHER READING

The books listed below were used by the author during his research. None of them are available from Stenlake Publishing. Those interested in finding out more are advised to contact their local bookshop or reference library.

Gifford, John; McWilliam, Colin; Walker, David; & Wilson, Christopher, *The Buildings of Scotland: Edinburgh*, 1984
Harris, Stuart, 'The Fortifications and Siege of Leith', *Proceedings of the Society of Antiquaries of Scotland*, 1991
Hunter, D. L. G., *Edinburgh's Transport, The Early Years*, 1992
Irons, James Campbell, *Leith and its Antiquities*, 1897
Marshall, James Scott, *The Life and Times of Leith*, 1985
McKerracher, A. C., 'The Edinburgh Bushrangers', *Scots Magazine*, September 1986
Smith, W. A. C., & Anderson, Paul, *An Illustrated History of Edinburgh's Railways*, 1995
Vacha, Robert, 'Leith at War', series of articles in *Evening Dispatch*, 1960
Wallace, Joyce, *Traditions of Trinity and Leith*, 1985
Wallace, Joyce, *Further Traditions of Trinity and Leith*, 1990
Moubray House Press, *Faces of Leith*, 1986

INTRODUCTION

The prefix 'Inver', which means 'at the mouth of', got stranded upstream leaving the Water of Leith to flow into the Forth at a town known simply as Leith. This broken convention somehow typifies the unique, thrawn character of a place that has, throughout its existence, been sandwiched between the Devil (Edinburgh) and the deep blue sea.

As the port for the nation's capital, Leith saw the arrival or departure of many royal persons. Usually they just passed through, but Mary, Queen of Scots' mother, Marie de Guise, acting as Queen Regent, established a residence there and based French troops in the port. These were intended to protect the Catholic throne, but in 1560 a Protestant army consisting mainly of Englishmen besieged them behind their defences while Scots stood on the sidelines and egged on their own particular cause. Stuck in the middle of someone else's fight, Leithers were shot at and starved until Marie de Guise died and the French left. The following year Mary, Queen of Scots stepped ashore at Leith and moved on to Edinburgh to claim her throne.

Edinburgh's ancient burghal status gave it peculiar rights over Leith, which it held in thrall until 1833 when, under the Burgh Reform Act, the port became independent. It developed its own civic institutions, police and fire services, and installed electric trams which were vastly superior to the capital's cable cars. But while Leith exulted in its freedom, Edinburgh pushed through a series of Municipal Extension Acts which progressively expanded the city's limits until it surrounded Leith, effectively putting it under siege again. At least no one was shooting, but in 1919 the capital promoted another extension, this time to take over the port. A plebiscite, suggested by the *Leith Observer*, was held and the vast majority of Leith's voters opposed amalgamation with Edinburgh. It was to no avail, since Parliament approved Edinburgh's Act and in October 1920 Leith was absorbed into the city.

Leith was, by this time, a place of industry, docks, warehouses and tightly packed, densely populated streets of tenements. Improvements were needed, but the capital did little with its new acquisition until after the Second World War when the planners moved in, knocked down Leith's character and replaced it with concrete.

For half a century the proud old port absorbed the knocks, but then quite suddenly in the 1980s and 90s it became the smart place to be. Surviving old buildings began to be redeveloped and new blocks of flats started to go up, a process that has accelerated through the property boom at the start of the twenty-first century. The port is busy again too as Scotland's commercial pendulum has swung back to the east, and as if to emphasise its pivotal place in national politics, the Scottish Executive has established its offices at the docks, thus making Leith a place of government. So who took over whom?

The glossy new Leith, however, exists alongside another community, one the Sunday supplement journalists only write about when they want to shock with a story about prostitution, drugs or Irvine Welsh and *Trainspotting*. This other Leith is evident in 'To Let' signs over the doors of empty shops, and bus queues made up of people of all ages and from every ethnic group clutching shopping bags from cut-price supermarkets. So behind the mask the old Leith still exists, still stoical, full of character and preserving Leith's historic image as a place of contrasts.

A studio setting for a late nineteenth century picture of Newhaven life.

So seamlessly are Leith and Edinburgh joined that there is now nothing on Leith Walk to tell people when they are leaving or arriving in port or city, although for the fifteen years before the amalgamation there was one very obvious indication of change at Pilrig. After 1905, passengers had to transfer here between Leith's state-of-the-art electric trams and Edinburgh's less than successful cable cars. The whole thing was a mess, known at the time as the 'Pilrig muddle'. People often preferred just to walk 'The Walk' instead of hanging about waiting for one tram or another. After the takeover, Edinburgh conceded the superiority of electric trams, but for a while the muddle, if anything, got more muddled. The worn out cable car system was discontinued in January 1921, but electrification of Edinburgh's tramways was not completed until June 1922, and so for that year and a half buses ran between Pilrig and the city centre. In this view, taken thirty years later, a tram runs unhindered past the old Pilrig termini. Iona Street is on the right and the tram tracks curving off to the left are going to and from Pilrig Street.

Balfour Street, seen here looking towards Leith Walk, was formerly the avenue that led from Pilrig House to The Walk. It was once lined with beech trees, but these were felled in the 1860s and the land feued for tenement housing by the then Laird of Pilrig, John Mackintosh Balfour-Melville. He was originally plain Mr Balfour, but added the Melville part of his name after inheriting Mount Melville Estate to the east of St Andrews. These fine, dressed rubble tenements are on the north side of the street and have some interesting architectural details including arched doorways and chimneys corbelled out from first floor level. Other chunks of the Pilrig Estate were feued at much the same time to provide much-needed tenement housing for working people. These tenements did not, initially, have water piped to the upper floors because of insufficient pressure, a problem that was only rectified after the supply companies serving Edinburgh and Leith amalgamated.

This 1950s view of the foot of The Walk was taken from the top deck of a tram just outside Leith depot, where the tracks in the right foreground are heading. Once inside, these fanned out to provide parking space for trams when not in use. There were also repair facilities, with pits between the rails where engineers could work underneath the vehicles. The depot became an integral part of Edinburgh's expanded tram system after 1920, but shut in 1956 as the system was progressively cut back prior to closure. The picture also gives a good view of the now-demolished railway bridge. It was built in the 1890s by the Caledonian Railway in connection with the extension of its lines from Newhaven to Seafield. When first proposed, these tracks formed part of a scheme that could have provided Edinburgh with an extensive suburban network. It would have involved massive engineering work including cut and cover tunnels under the city and a link from west to east across Leith, but while the port was keen, the city was not, and only the Leith lines went ahead with impressive bridges here and across Pilrig Road.

The priority for early railway companies was the movement of goods, especially coal: catering for passengers was often just tacked on as an afterthought. Thus, by 1900, three long and winding railway lines had been laid into Leith docks and although they all offered passenger services, none could be described as quick, central or convenient. The North British Railway sought to remedy this by building a large new station at the foot of The Walk called Leith Central. It opened in July 1903. Trains ran on suburban routes around Edinburgh, and also to stations in Dundee and Glasgow, but the principal service was the five minute run to Edinburgh Waverley known as the 'penny jump'. For a while these trains prospered, but after 1922 when electric trams were able to run uninterrupted up The Walk to the city centre demand declined. Passenger services ceased in 1952. The grand station was used as a depot for twenty years until it was abandoned and, in 1989, demolished.

The busy junction at the foot of Leith Walk was the meeting place of five roads: The Walk, Great Junction Street, Kirkgate, Constitution Street (seen here in 1954 with a tram heading down towards Bernard Street) and Duke Street. These days of course road-users have only four streets to choose from because Kirkgate was pedestrianised in a 1965 redevelopment scheme. The buildings facing the camera are regarded as being in Duke Street, although they face directly up Leith Walk. There is an almost timeless quality about the shops that seem to have always occupied them: Woolworths, and to its left Smith & Bowman's pharmacy, still a chemists today, although the name has changed. In front of it is one of Leith's best-known landmarks, the statue of Queen Victoria, which was made by sculptor John Stevenson Rhind and erected in 1907. It became a favourite place for men to gather and while away some time putting the world to rights and debating the great issues of the day. Leith's politics have always been radical and often at variance with those of the city.

Duke Street is seen here looking back towards the foot of The Walk in 1953 with a tram on its way from Craigentinny to Corstorphine. This section of the street was so narrow that trams going in both directions had to use a single track. The advertising hoardings facing the camera are on the gable of a tenement that was built on the line of Glover Street. At the time this picture was taken it was the surviving rump of what had originally been a longer thoroughfare running roughly parallel with Leith Walk, and which was virtually obliterated when Leith Central station was erected. Now of course the station has been demolished, along with everything that can be seen to the left in this picture. Glover Street has disappeared altogether, and the site is now mainly occupied by a Scotmid supermarket. Included amongst its services is a travel agent's which entices Leithers to sample a range of exotic destinations infinitely more exciting than that offered by the local train to Edinburgh!

Leith dealt in wine, spirits and other commodities which required barrels, and so there were a number of cooperages in the town, one of which appears to be shown in this picture. Written on the reverse are the initials ND&S, a somewhat cryptic clue but one that almost certainly refers to Neil Drysdale & Son, whose cooperage was in Easter Road at the corner of St Clair Avenue. The cooper here is working at a chiming machine – a chime is the protruding rim of a barrel which was formed by this machine after the staves had been assembled and banded together. Drysdale's closed down as new forms of packaging, faster transport and better storage reduced the need for barrels. There is now no trace of the former works, but across the road from where the cooperage used to be is a clue to its former existence – a pub called the Coopers' Rest. One business which may well have used Drysdale's barrels was the Buttercup Dairy, whose headquarters was at the foot of Easter Road. The company was founded in 1909 and grew to operate a chain of over 250 spotlessly clean shops throughout Scotland and the North of England.

Lochend Road School was built by Leith School Board to the designs of George Craig, an architect who was responsible for a number of school buildings in the port. The foundation stone was laid in October 1885 and the school opened in January 1887. An indication of its size can be gauged from the fact that over 1,000 children had to be evacuated when a fire was discovered in 1928. The blaze broke out in an attic room and the school was alerted by the sewing teacher who blew on the fire whistle to raise the alarm – there was a whistle on every floor for such a purpose. If this sounds rudimentary, it was clearly just one element of a fire safety regime that must have included practice drills, because the children were all evacuated safely, and without panic, in under two minutes. That schoolchildren at the time were well-drilled is borne out by another fire, in 1923, when 1,500 children at Bonnington Road School were evacuated in under three minutes. Lochend Road School was later used as an annexe of Leith Academy Secondary School.

Typically people living in old Leith crowded together in closely packed tenements, but there were pockets of more upmarket dwellings like these in Cornhill Terrace in the area between Lochend Road and Restalrig Road. This had formerly been part of the grounds of Hermitage House, a mansion erected in 1754 and boasting, as one of its many attractions, running water. Perched on the high ground overlooking the port, the occupants of the house would have had the opportunity to observe its expansion in the nineteenth century, and with the city also marching towards it from the south the small estate was sold off in chunks for housing. The first parcel of land was disposed of in the late 1860s to the Edinburgh Co-operative Building Company which built little houses in distinctive rows all named after trees or woods. Cornhill Terrace, and other streets to the south of these rows, were erected a few years later, and by the 1880s the big house had been demolished and the whole area transformed into built-up suburbia.

The Edinburgh & Dalkeith Railway was one of the earliest railways in Scotland, and like other early lines was made to move coal. Prior to this, coal was transported into Edinburgh by carters, rogues who could be relied on for little other than their skill at overcharging and giving short measure. The railway was completed from Lugton, near Dalkeith, to the St Leonard's area in 1831, and although a branch had reached Seafield by 1832 its completion to Leith was delayed until 1836. As well as coal, the line carried grain and catered for passengers. It was bought in 1845 by the North British Railway (NBR) which upgraded it, but by the early twentieth century coal owners had become unhappy with bottlenecks on the tracks leading into Leith docks and sought improvements. These were eventually implemented by the NBR between 1913 and 1915, transforming the Seafield area with embankments and bridges. This one was built across Seafield Place, which was also the terminus for the No. 12 tram from Corstorphine before the route was extended to Joppa. Behind the trams and railway bridge are the maltings of Thomas Bernard & Co. Ltd.

The old Leith Academy is one of the most distinctive buildings on the periphery of the Links, that ancient piece of common land that has somehow managed to survive the urban advance and remains a priceless open space in Leith's crowded townscape. These youngsters from the school, photographed in 1929, are dressed for a pageant held in Princes Street Gardens to celebrate Edinburgh's 600th year. Schoolchildren from all over the city took part, re-enacting moments from Scottish history; these boys showed off one aspect of Leith's historical past – golf. The game has since become a worldwide phenomenon, but there is strong evidence to suggest that its rules were first set down by golfers who played on Leith Links, and despite contrary claims emanating from St Andrews, and more recently Holland, Leith has a good claim to be the true home of golf. Leith Academy replaced the earlier Leith High School building in the 1890s, and when a new secondary school was erected in the 1930s the old building became Leith Primary School.

It seems extraordinary to modern perceptions that golf could have been played on an area like the Links which was being used at the same time for many other purposes. People went there to hang out their washing, graze animals and hone their military skills, but despite this Leithers have used the Links as a place of recreation throughout the centuries. The golfers eventually had to find other locations, as did the once-festive Leith Races which had degenerated into a spectacle of antisocial behaviour and drunkenness before their move to Musselburgh. This was in marked contrast to the Leith Games, which attracted large numbers of people to participate in or watch a variety of athletic and sporting events, while at the same time traders and performers set up fairground stalls to entertain the crowds. The games ceased when the rough natural terrain was levelled and drained in the late nineteenth century, and the organisers baulked at the idea of having to repair any damage. Nevertheless, as this picture from 1937 shows, the Links continued to provide an ideal location for fairground rides and sideshows.

The area to the north of the Links was sandwiched between parkland on one side and the docks on the other. Here the Scottish Co-operative Wholesale Society had a large distribution depot, and other commercial and industrial premises jostled for space with tenements. At least one woman had cause to regret living here during the Second World War when an artillery shell, fired to warn a trawler it was approaching a minefield, ricocheted off the water, flew over the dock sheds and smashed through her flat in Salamander Street. The street was named after a French ship gifted to the Scottish nation in 1537, and other street names here – Baltic, Cadiz and Elbe – also reflect the port's maritime and trading links. Another reminder of Leith's trading history is the corn exchange, built in the early 1860s on the corner of Baltic Street and Constitution Street, the site of an old naval yard. These days the word 'corn' has become associated with maize, or sweetcorn, but it is really a catch-all for any grain and used to describe the dominant one in an area, be it wheat, barley, or – as was the case in much of Scotland – oats.

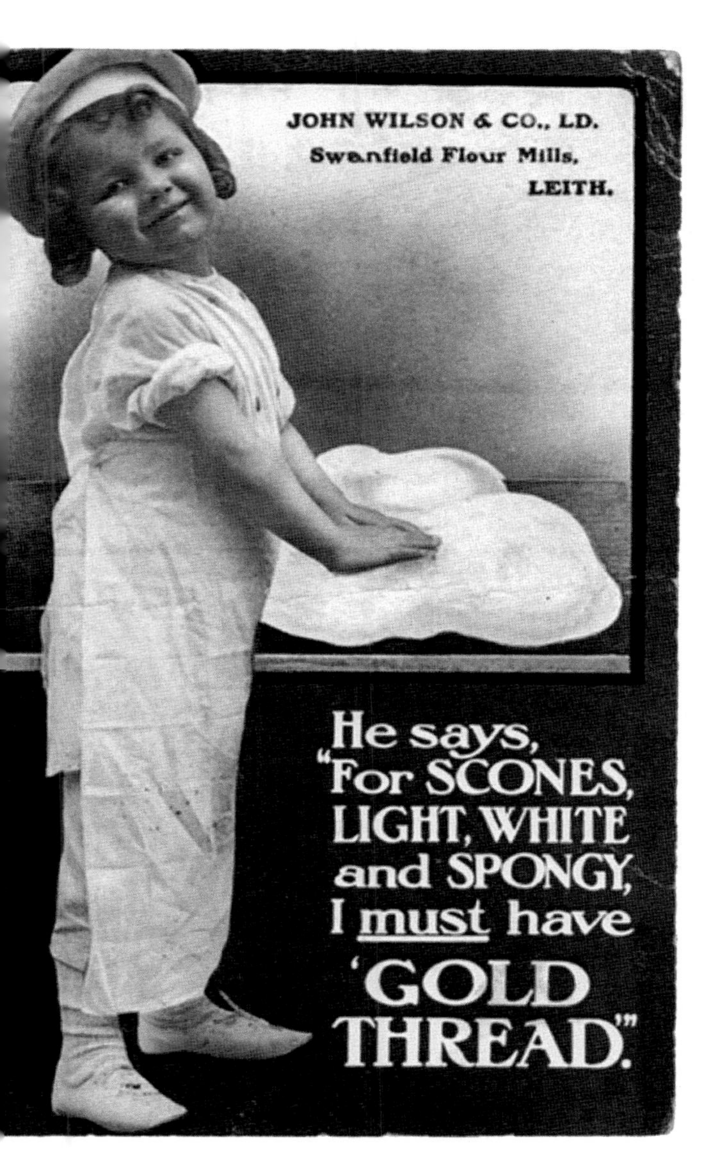

As a market, Leith's corn exchange was of huge importance to the Scottish grain trade, often setting the benchmark in prices. It did this because here traders could compare home-grown grain from East and Mid Lothian – the best in the country – with imported grain coming in through the docks. With the best grain being traded at its corn exchange, Leith became one the country's most important milling centres with a number of large operations packed into a relatively small area. Here the Scottish Co-operative Wholesale Society (SCWS) set up their huge Chancelot Mills, which predominantly milled wheat flour but were also used for other grains. The SCWS also bought Junction Mill at the Bowling Green area of Bonnington where it concentrated on milling oatmeal. That mill's former owner, John Inglis & Sons Ltd., also carried on milling oats at its mill in Bonnington Road and remained in business until the large conglomerates squeezed out the small independent millers. John Wilson & Co.'s Swanfield Mill was also in the Bonnington area.

Leith's milling activities are again emphasised by the printed bag for Snowpeak Flour displayed on the board in front of this group of white-clad women. They look like mill-workers – indeed one lady in the second row looks as if she has been hit by a dollop of flour – but appearances can be deceiving. The initials J&J T&SL on the board in front of the group are most likely to refer to wholesale provision merchants John & James Tod & Sons Ltd. The company originated as a small grocery business which was started in Dalkeith in 1750, passing through the generations until 1841 when the owner's grandsons John and James Tod took it over. They disposed of the retail side, dispensed with the licence to sell liquor and concentrated on building up the wholesale business. Tod's moved to Mitchell Street in Leith in 1877, and at the time this picture was taken the company was also operating out of premises in Charlotte Street, a name that was later changed to Queen Charlotte Street to avoid confusion with Charlotte Square in Edinburgh. Part of the firm's expansion came as a result of taking over other businesses, but in 1946 Tod's was itself taken over when it became part of the Beecham group of companies.

Constitution Street and Bernard Street, the latter seen here looking east, were creations of the late eighteenth century, and many old wynds and closes disappeared to make way for them. In the case of Bernard Street the narrow Weigh-house Wynd was replaced by a wide, generously proportioned thoroughfare. The tramlines in the foreground are turning out of Constitution Street into Bernard Street, which was used as a tram terminus, the first tram to operate in Leith running from here to and from Haymarket along Leith Walk and Princes Street. It was horse-drawn and operated by a private company which ran trams throughout Edinburgh and Leith before the city and port introduced their separate municipal systems. In the right foreground is the statue of Rabbie Burns erected in 1898, one of a surprisingly small number of such memorials to a poet who is held in such esteem and affection throughout the country. Standing out amongst the street's no-nonsense four-square Scottish buildings is a distinctive domed structure about halfway down on the left-hand side. This was built as the Leith Bank in 1806 by the architect John Paterson.

Tolbooth Wynd was full of character and a hive of activity. It was one of Leith's older streets, but had been redeveloped in the nineteenth century, and so by the 1960s the buildings were not particularly special when they were demolished in another redevelopment. The structures that replaced them have almost universally failed to live up to the claims that were made for them. Certainly Linksview House, an uninspiring block of flats set back from the line of Tollbooth Wynd, cannot, at least from the lower floors, live up to its name. In fairness, the architects and planners of the time faced some daunting problems. The country was still recovering from a world war, people wanted to see their lot improved and many old buildings were in such poor condition that they had to be pulled down before they fell down. Such was the fate of a four-storey tenement in Market Street, just off Tolbooth Wynd, in October 1932. The front wall started to bulge one evening and the following morning it collapsed. Fortunately the delay had given some warning of impending structural failure and so no one was hurt, but nine families were made homeless.

Driven by regenerative zeal, Scotland's town planners of the 1960s redeveloped many old towns. The loss of buildings was sad, but not always bad, and something was usually built to replace them. Despite this, the loss of what made communities tick was irreplaceable. Arguably Leith suffered more than most communities as people were dispersed to schemes miles away on the edge of the city. Kirkgate was the beating heart of old Leith, a busy, bustling thoroughfare with a warren of little streets, pends and closes leading off it. One of its many attractions was the New Gaiety Theatre which put on a range of performances from Shakespearean drama to the annual pantomime – a must for all Leith children, some of whom took part. These 'Leith Little Lassies' appear to have been an annual attraction before the First World War, and this group were in the 1910–11 panto, *The Dolls' Frolic* by John Darlison. The New Kirkgate has no such fun, no Gaiety Theatre and no panto, and the vibrant life of the old street has gone, probably forever.

The large domed building in the centre of this view of Great Junction Street was erected by the Leith Provident Co-operative Society in 1911. Although the Rochdale Friendly Co-operative Society, set up in 1832, is regarded as the first true co-op, Scotland played a leading role in the co-operative movement. A number of small friendly and victualling societies predated the Rochdale pioneers, and many more were set up following the Friendly Societies Act of 1834. Edinburgh's St Cuthbert's Co-operative Association was established in 1859, just before the peak of Scottish registrations in the 1860s, but Leith's desire to be independent of its city neighbour even extended to the world of co-operative trading. Three societies tried and failed to become established before Leith Provident opened its first store at 147 Great Junction Street on 27 May 1878. The following year the society moved to a shop in Bonnington Road and then in 1881 purchased an old glass factory in Bangor Road, adapting it to become its centre of operations. After that its stores spread across the whole of Leith, an expansion which included a considerable and conspicuous presence on Great Junction Street where it all began.

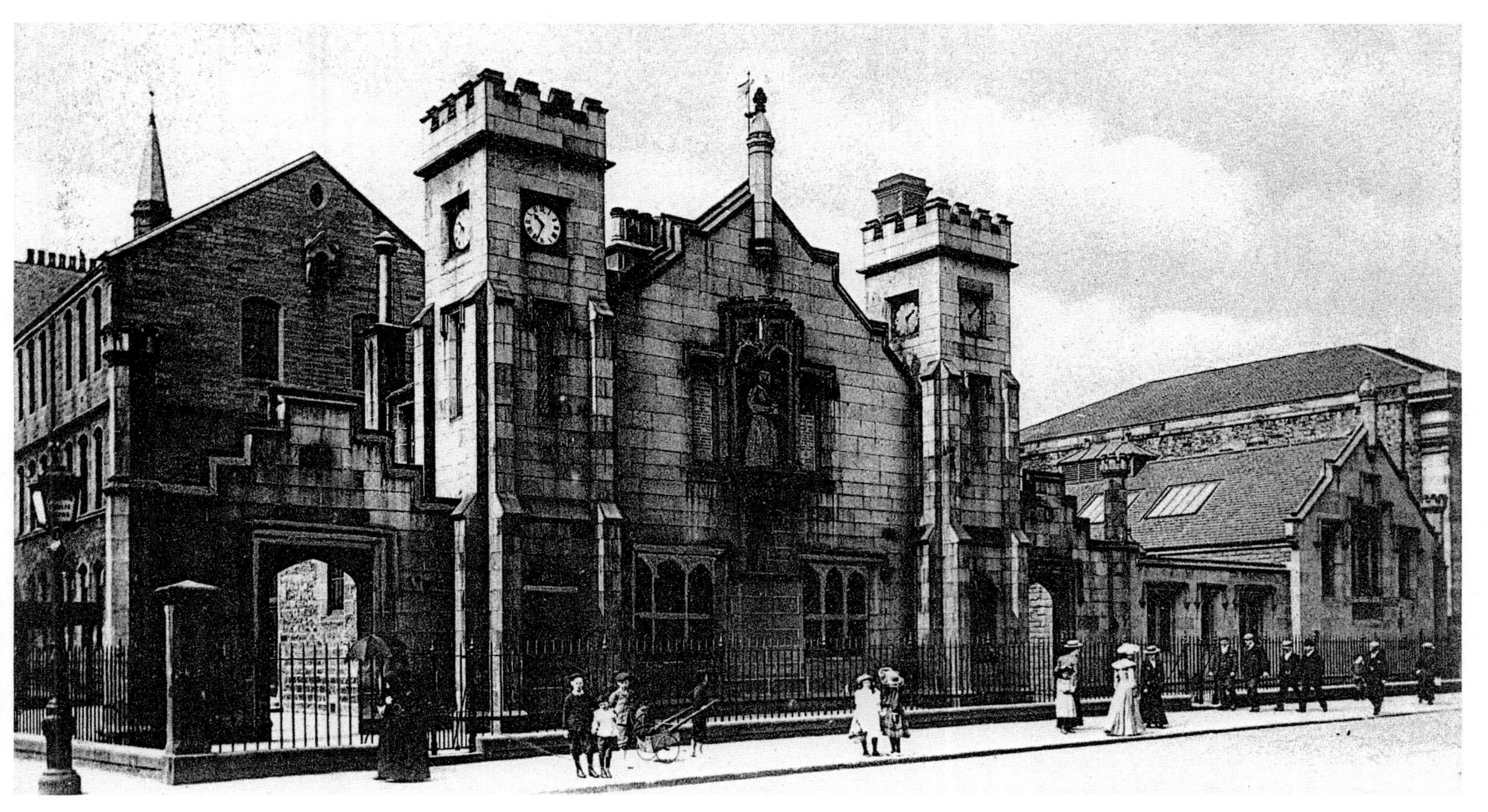

The Education Act of 1872 charged local authorities with providing schools and made it compulsory for children aged between five and thirteen to attend. Leith School Board was set up to implement the Act in the burgh. It inherited a motley collection of schools which catered for a minority of the port's children and taught them in a variety of ways. One of these was Dr Bell's school in Great Junction Street. This used the 'Madras system', in which a small staff of adult teachers was assisted by monitors – senior pupils who helped the younger children. The original school building was erected in 1839, the extension on the left was added in 1892, while the small building on the right is a swimming pool dating from 1896. Dr Bell's later became known as Junction Road School although the street has never been officially named Junction Road! Another institution in Great Junction Street with an educational function, St James Episcopal Hall and School, can be seen at the right-hand edge of the picture on the facing page. It has now been demolished to be replaced with flats featuring the seemingly inevitable penthouses.

Leith Hospital is now closed and like much of old Leith is finding a new purpose as flats. The first of the large complex of buildings that made up the hospital was the one on the right, situated in Mill Lane. Carved below the entrance portico is the date 1850 in Roman numerals. Designed by the architect Peter Hamilton, the building originally had two storeys, but was later raised to three. The structure to its left, with the mansard roof, was erected *c.*1875 and also had a storey added a few years later. A further extension and a nurses' home were added by the early twentieth century.

This drawing, possibly by the architect George Simpson, shows the children's hospital which was added to the complex after the First World War. It was in fact Leith's war memorial, and was somehow typical of the town and its people to eschew a grandiose cenotaph and instead raise funds for something practical, with a social purpose. In January 1927 the hospital was opened by the Secretary of State for Scotland, the Rt. Hon. Sir John Gilmour. The building faces Taylor Gardens which had formerly been the site of a poorhouse fronting onto Great Junction Street. A number of hospitals around the country took over poorhouses or their former sites.

LEITH WAR MEMORIAL CHILDREN'S HOSPITAL

When Leith School Board assumed responsibility for the provision of universal education it faced a massive task. Existing school buildings were hopelessly inadequate for the thousands of children who had previously been left out of the system, so a number of large new schools had to be built. The architect George Craig designed many of them, including Lochend Road School on page 11 and the austere-looking Couper Street School which opened in November 1890. It had accommodation for 1,900 pupils of all ages, but as subsequent Education Acts raised the school leaving age it became a primary school and a new junior secondary was built in nearby North Junction Street.

The new school, also designed by George Craig, was named the David Kilpatrick School after the minister of Newhaven Free Church who was chairman of the Leith School Board when building started in September 1915. Work was completed in September 1917, but with the First World War in full swing the building was needed for purposes other than education, and was used as such until the start of the school year in September 1919. DK's, as the school was known locally, came close to an even greater disruption during the Second World War when a landmine hit the adjacent town hall.

With boats operating out of Granton, the Edinburgh, Leith & Granton Railway (EL&G) pioneered travel across the Forth, journeys that only became practical wholly by rail when the Forth Bridge opened in 1890. The EL&G line from Scotland Street to Granton Harbour was opened in February 1846, and extended at the Edinburgh end through a tunnel to Princes Street in 1847. Three months after reaching Granton another branch of the line was opened running down beside the Water of Leith to a station called Leith North, beside Commercial Street. The tracks carried on across Commercial Street to the docks. In 1862 the EL&G was taken over by the North British Railway and six years later it engineered a new route out of Waverley station which joined up with the Leith branch line near Warriston cemetery, and with the Granton branch at Trinity. At the same time it opened a new station called Junction Road which was raised up on stilts from the valley below. Its overgrown platforms can be seen in this picture from 1960, taken thirteen years after the last passenger train used it. Leith North, renamed Leith Citadel in 1952, continued to handle a daily fish train until 1968.

Vessels navigating the Water of Leith and requiring 'clear air draught' were halted by Junction Bridge, although boats without masts or superstructure could carry on beyond the bridge if the tide was right and the depth of water adequate. This (somewhat fuzzy) view from the tenement flats erected at the corner of Ferry Road in 1901 shows the river looking north and gives a splendid impression of what industrial Leith once looked like. On the east bank of the river are the sheds and chimneys of Hawthorn's yard. The company, one of the foremost engineering works in Leith, built small ships like the one tied up alongside here. The building berths were situated behind the sheds at the bend of the river and angled so that boats were launched along the river rather than across it. The company also built railway locomotives. Next to Hawthorn's yard was the wharf from where W Graham-Yooll & Co. traded in a variety of oils and dyes, as well as building materials and other commodities.

Yooll's Wharf, at the foot of Sheriff Brae, was just upstream of the riverfront street known as Coalhill, a term defined in a nineteenth century *Glossary of Scotch Mining Terms* as 'ground occupied at a pithead or mine-mouth for colliery purposes'. The term was also used to describe the binging ground at a port or railhead where coal was sold for onward shipping. Coalhill was therefore Leith's former coal wharf and the name has stuck. It was upstream of the lifting bridge from which this picture of the river was taken. The bridge connected Sandport with the Shore, which can be seen in the distance beyond the next crossing downstream, the Bernard Street Bridge. The boat on the left is sitting alongside a warehouse and wharf used for many years by I. C. Johnston & Co. who traded in cement. The large building behind it was a bonded warehouse used by wine wholesalers Innes & Grieve, who also traded in their own *Uam-Var* brand of whisky (no, I've never heard of it either!). Had it survived, this fine building, with its ornate Dutch gable, would have been a prime candidate for residential conversion. The building beyond it, the Cooperage, has been turned into flats.

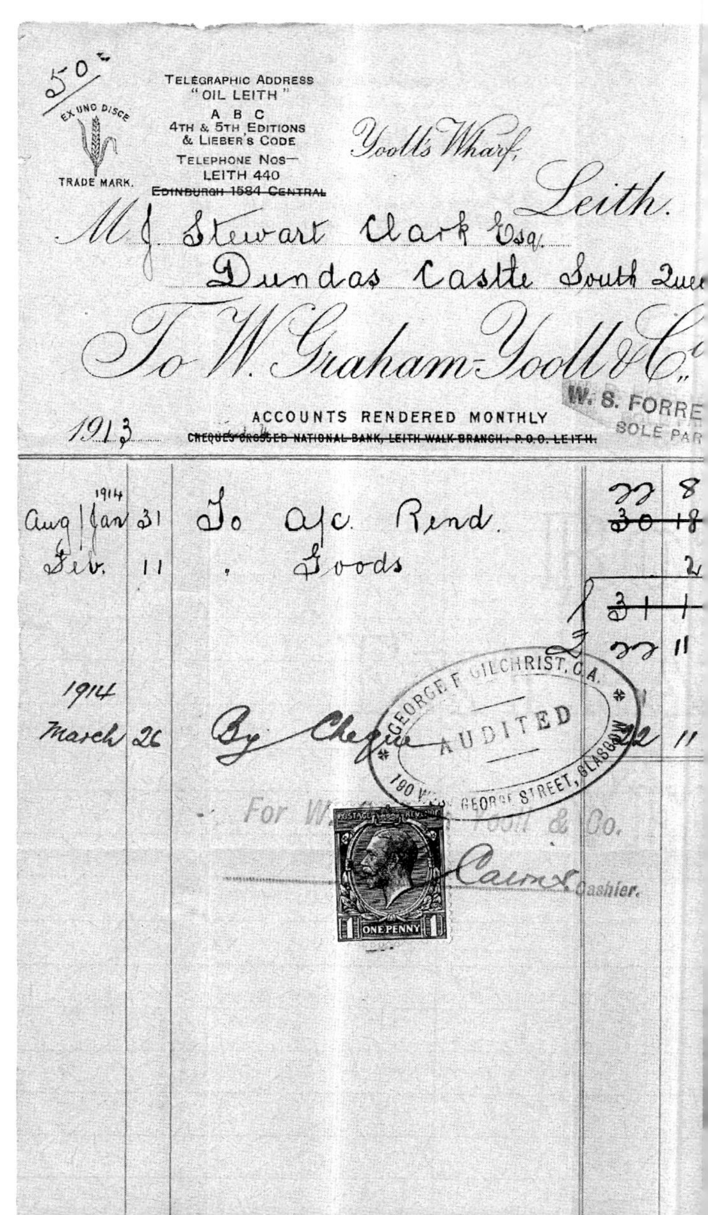

50

EX UNO DISCE
TRADE MARK.

TELEGRAPHIC ADDRESS
"OIL LEITH"
A B C
4TH & 5TH EDITIONS
& LIEBER'S CODE
TELEPHONE NOS—
LEITH 440
~~EDINBURGH 1584 CENTRAL~~

Yooll's Wharf,
Leith.

M J. Stewart Clark Esq.
Dundas Castle South Quee

To W. Graham-Yooll & Co.

W. S. FORRE
SOLE PAR

1913

ACCOUNTS RENDERED MONTHLY
~~CHEQUES CROSSED NATIONAL BANK, LEITH WALK BRANCH; P.O.O. LEITH.~~

Date		Particulars	£	s.
1914 Aug / Jan	31	To a/c Rend.	33 / ~~30~~	8 / ~~18~~
Feb.	11	" Goods		2
			~~31~~	~~1~~
			33	11
1914 March	26	By Cheque	33	11

GEORGE F. GILCHRIST, C.A.
AUDITED
190 W. GEORGE STREET, GLASGOW

For W. Graham Yooll & Co.
ONE PENNY
Cairns Cashier.

Navigation up the Water of Leith was made possible by opening bridges, but the old swing bridge which connected Bernard Street and Commercial Street restricted the development of road traffic because it was unsuitable for tram rails. This difficulty was overcome when the bridge was closed in 1897 and replaced the following year by a new one built by Sir William Armstrong's Newcastle-based engineering company. At the time Edinburgh still hoped to persuade Leith to install cable cars as part of an extended system, but Leith's decision to buy out the privately run horse-drawn trams and go electric created further problems at the Bernard Street Bridge. The electric cables had to be carried over the bridge and to do this bow-shaped gantries were fitted so that the cables could move with the bridge and realign exactly. When the bridge was open to river traffic the current was cut off, thus depriving trams of power, and for safety the tracks were fitted with mechanisms known as 'trap points' which stopped runaway trams from rolling off the ends of the rails and into the water.

As a waterfront setting the Shore is hard to equal, but until recently it was regarded as seedy, and certainly not the kind of place that tourists should be encouraged to go to. Not now. The sailors' home, on the left, where indigent mariners could rest and recuperate is now an upmarket hotel, and the distinctive round signal tower hosts a high-class restaurant. To its right is John Cran's Albert Engine Works which was later taken over by ship repairers George Brown & Sons. The top floor of the building has been taken off and the next floor down modified, but Brown's are still there. The firm still offers a ship repair service, and the smell and sound of metal being fabricated is faintly reassuring when set against Leith's glossy, frothy consumer image. On the right of the picture are some steam lighters of the Leith, Hull & Hamburg Steam Packet Company. These little vessels were distinctive in a couple of ways: they had unusually tall, slender funnels and were named with single letters of the alphabet – facing camera is *A* with what appears to be *X* alongside her. They were used up until the 1920s for coastal shipping and on a regular run through the Forth & Clyde Canal to Port Dundas in Glasgow.

As its name implies, the Leith, Hull & Hamburg Steam Packet Co. did not confine its activities to coastal waters, but traded extensively with northern Europe. One of its ships, seen here in Leith, was the 1,286-ton *Gothland*. She was built in 1932 by Henry Robb, Leith's last and largest shipbuilder, and operated on a regular run to and from Hamburg. When the Second World War broke out two things happened: the company changed its name to the Currie Line (having Hamburg in the title was potentially embarrassing) and *Gothland* was requisitioned by the Admiralty. It initially used her to run cargoes to the Mediterranean, but had to install extra bunker capacity before she could undertake such long journeys. In 1941 she went to Plymouth to be fitted out as a convoy rescue ship. Her job was to sit at the tail of convoys and when ships were sunk to go to the assistance of their crews. She had to locate the men in the water and, with ladders and scrambling nets slung over the side, stop and take them on board, all the time a sitting target. The little *Gothland* became a legend of the Atlantic convoys, even doing what the *Titanic* couldn't do, hitting an iceberg and staying afloat. They built good ships in Leith!

The *Sirius*, the first steam vessel to cross the Atlantic, was built in Leith by Robert Menzies & Sons, but by the 1930s, when this photograph of the docks was taken, the company was concentrating on repair work at the yard in the centre of the picture. The port was originally just a tidally restricted river harbour to which access was further impeded by a troublesome sand bar, but through the nineteenth and twentieth centuries the docks were developed into a large deep-water complex. The first major works, dating from 1806 and 1817, were latterly known as the East and West Old Docks, and can be seen beyond the dock gates on the left. Both docks were infilled in the 1990s and the Scottish Executive offices built on the reclaimed ground. Alongside these docks, on the right of this picture, was the Victoria Dock which was completed in 1852. These developments on the west bank of the river were followed on the east bank by the Albert, Edinburgh, and Imperial Docks made in 1865, 1881 and 1902 respectively. Newhaven is in the distance, with Granton Harbour beyond, a view that has been transformed in recent years.

With each successive dock development Leith's waterfront and harbour was pushed towards the deeper water of the Firth of Forth. Long piers were built out on both sides of the dredged approach channel to the docks to delineate and protect it. The West Pier is seen behind the *St Fergus*, a ship built by Hawthorn & Co. in 1913 for service in the wild waters of the Orkney and Shetland Islands. The piers also provided young boys – at least those who were inclined to risk life and limb in pursuit of a challenge – with a place to dive and swim off. In 1942 the piers were largely superseded by the construction of substantial breakwaters which curved from east and west towards each other to create a protected dock entrance. This gap was closed in 1955 and dock gates installed, completing an entirely man-made shoreline between Seafield and Newhaven. The gates controlled the water level in all the docks and up the Water of Leith, as well as enclosing the huge Western Harbour. Its acres of reclaimed ground were intended for docks and industry, but now the Ocean Terminal development with the former Royal Yacht *Britannia* alongside, and high-rise flats with expensive-sounding names, have transformed them into a tourist destination and desirable living space.

On the left of this view, looking east along Commercial Street towards the Bernard Street Bridge, is the Customs House, which is no longer used for its original purpose but remains one of Leith's most distinctive Georgian buildings. It was erected in 1812 to the designs of Edinburgh architect Robert Reid on a quayside site that had previously been used for boat-building. The docks that superseded the old riverside quays lay behind Commercial Street and access to them was by way of Dock Place, which leads off to the left beside the Customs House. With valuable excise-earning commodities going in and out, the dock gates were manned for security purposes by police. Two sergeants were on duty one February night in 1881 when two men aroused their suspicions. They arrested them and were taking them in for questioning when their instincts were suddenly and shockingly proved right: the men drew pistols and shot the sergeants. Leaving the officers wounded, their attackers ran off along Commercial Street with a young constable hot on their tail.

The gunmen approached the dock gates on the left of this picture where two other policemen called on them to stop, but were also fired on. One was hit. The local beat constable joined the chase. He cornered one of the men near Admiralty Street and bravely moved to arrest him, but the man shot himself dead. His accomplice was trapped by the other policemen at what is now Hopefield Terrace and also tried to commit suicide, but his gun failed and he was arrested. Throughout the subsequent questioning and trial he remained silent as to his true identity, but the belief was that he and his partner in crime were Australian bushrangers who were trying their luck in the old country after the police Down Under had made life too hot for them. It seems the Leith police made life even hotter. Commercial Street looks different now. The splendid warehouses, designed *c.*1810 by John Paterson, resident engineer of the Leith Docks, have been converted into flats, and the offices of the Scottish Executive now stand on the infilled docks behind them. There is of course no connection between the people who work there and armed robbery!

The austere, functional architecture of the dockside warehouses was typical of the buildings along Commercial Street which, true to its name, was a place where commerce and industry ruled. It is seen here on the left with North Junction Street, the continuation of Great Junction Street, to the right. Behind the gaunt building at the gushet is Leith Flour Mills, also known as North Leith Mills, a huge structure built for commerce and not beauty. A. & R. Tod, the firm that ran it, was set up by Alexander and Robert Tod, brothers of John and James, whose wholesale grocery business is described on page 18. One of Edinburgh's distinctive police boxes is just to the left of the tramcar. At the left-hand edge of the picture, behind the 'Cars Stop by Request' sign, is the entrance to the old Caledonian Railway station which at various times was known as Leith, Leith North and North Leith. This was of course a different station to the North Leith station of the Caley's great rivals, the North British Railway, which was at the Citadel, further east along Commercial Street (see page 26).

Finding a route to the docks through Edinburgh and Leith's congested townscapes was not easy for the Caledonian Railway. This Glasgow-based company was always struggling in the east of Scotland to keep pace with Edinburgh's North British Railway (the reverse, of course, was true for the NBR in the west of Scotland). The Caley's main terminal in Edinburgh was at the west end of the city's principal street and was known, unsurprisingly, as Princes Street station. The route from there to Leith ran in a wide loop round by Crewe Toll, following Ferry Road for just over a mile and then cutting north to pass under Craighall Road about halfway along its length. Newhaven station was built beside the overbridge, and Craighall School, which later became Trinity Academy, was opened alongside it in 1894. Leith station, seen here from Lindsay Road, was a simple shed-like structure. The line was opened for passenger traffic in 1879, and although not the most direct route to the city it proved to be well-used, and was still being well-used in the early 1960s when services were stopped. New blocks of flats now occupy the surrounding area, but the station that might have been an asset for their occupants has gone.

Just as Leith was swallowed up by its larger neighbour, so the growing port town itself absorbed a number of proudly individual small communities like Bonnington. This village grew up beside the Water of Leith and thrived as a centre for milling and other industries that needed the abundant water supply obtainable from the river. One of these was a tannery sited in Newhaven Road opposite the tenement building in the centre of this picture. It was built to house the tannery workers and is called Burns Place after the industry's founder. A carved stone plaque on the face of the building bears the initials TB and the date 1890, while another plaque is carved with a sheep and the tools of the tanning and skinning trade. These are some of the few signs left to indicate that Bonnington was once a busy industrial village, although the mill name is kept alive by the business park opposite Burns Place. The tram seen here heading north from Pilrig is approaching Bonnington Bridge, which was jointly funded by Edinburgh and Leith and opened in 1903.

The municipal bowling greens at the southern end of Victoria Park can be seen through the railings on the left of this view of Newhaven Road. The park was created out of the grounds of Bonnington Park House, which can also be glimpsed through the trees on the left. It was occupied by Richard Raimes, a manufacturing chemist, and for a while local people rewarded his generosity by ignoring the park's patriotic name and referring to it as Raimes Park. Despite this the official name stuck. The house was later bought by a member of the Inglis family, whose oatmeal products are referred to on page 17, and the council subsequently purchased it from them. As well as its name, the park has another prominent royal memorial, a statue of King Edward VII made by John S. Rhind, the same sculptor who carved the statue to Queen Victoria at the foot of Leith Walk. He also made the memorial in Rosebank cemetery which commemorates the men of the 7th Royal Scots – Leith's Territorial Army battalion – who died in the terrible rail disaster at Gretna in 1915. The tram in the foreground is passing the end of Summerside Place where Bonnington United Free Church, with its imposing spire, once sat opposite a private bowling green at the intersection with Summerside Street.

Finding a name like Ferry Road in a port from which a number of ferries criss-crossed the Forth is hardly surprising, but it seems that the road name refers to none of these and is instead simply an extension of Edinburgh's Queensferry Road. The chemists on the corner of this tenement block was one of two in Leith run by Powell & Co., the other being at 23 Bernard Street. The company had an earlier association with Duncan, Flockhart & Co. who ran other shops in Edinburgh and also operated as manufacturing and wholesale chemists. There were a number of chemists at the foot of Ferry Road at the time this picture was taken; one owned by G. D. Thomson can be seen at the extreme left-hand edge of the picture, and there were two more on the other side of the road. These tenements, which can also be seen from the back on page 26, were situated diagonally across from the town hall and library. Construction work on these began in 1929 and they were opened by the Lord Provost of Edinburgh, Sir Thomas B. Whitson, in July 1932.

Chancelot Terrace, an upmarket tenement block on Ferry Road, was theoretically outside Leith because at this point the boundary ran along the middle of the road and W. F. Craigen's grocery shop was on the wrong – or Edinburgh – side of it. Young people making their mark on the world know no boundaries, however, and the scrawls on the stonework around the windows and doorway were as universal then as spray-painted graffiti are today. This modern medium upsets people because it does real damage, but the usual implement used by the youngsters who scribbled on these walls was a stick of chalk. Some of the scribblers, and possibly some of the chalk, may have come across the road from Holy Cross Academy, Leith's Catholic senior secondary school. The school was opened in 1907 in a house known as Afton Lodge. This had extensive grounds where a new school was later built, and the Afton name was given to one the school's three houses, the others being Chancelot and Hawthorn. Numbered amongst former pupils who achieved fame or fortune are Cardinal Gordon Gray and Hibs and Scotland footballer Pat Stanton.

These days pundits and punters alike refer to Hibernian Football Club as being a Leith team, but to be strictly (and boringly) accurate their Easter Road ground is actually on the Edinburgh side of the old boundary line. So strictly speaking Leith does not have a senior football team, but for a while it did: Leith Athletic. The club was founded in 1887 and for the next thirteen years or so had a somewhat nomadic existence, playing at Hawkhill Grounds, Bank Park and Beechwood Park. It moved to Chancelot Park about 1900 and remained there until 1923 when another thirteen years of travelling saw its team playing at Powderhall, Marine Gardens and finally Meadowbank, which the club made its home from 1936 to 1954 when it was wound up. With such a history, perhaps Leith Wanderers would have been a more appropriate name, and being constantly on the move may be one reason why the club never made an impact on the upper echelons of senior football. Despite these difficulties Leith Athletic were second division champions three times and runners-up on four other occasions. The team is seen in their black and white strips following success in the Scottish qualifying challenge cup in season 1905–06.

Local graffiti artists appear to have been practising copybook techniques with the street number of this branch of the Leith Provident Co-operative Society on the corner of the distinctive Anchorfield tenements. When they were built they looked out across the Forth, but the shoreline disappeared in 1955 when the Western Harbour was developed and from the 1960s the huge Chancelot Mill dominated the view. Its construction perpetuated the name of an earlier mill that, when built, was regarded by the trade as possibly the 'very handsomest flour mill in the world'. It was erected by the Scottish Co-operative Wholesale Society to provide flour to retail societies, such as Leith Provident, and was opened on 25 August 1894 by Mrs William Maxwell, wife of the SCWS president. She turned on the steam to start a 500 horsepower engine which drove milling machinery capable of producing forty sacks of flour an hour (although initially it was only required to mill up to twenty-five). The society's foresight in providing for such expansion was warmly applauded by the 800 or so people who turned up, not just to witness the ceremony but also to attend the 103rd quarterly meeting of the SCWS which was held at the mill.

For a nation that is so proud of its heritage, the Scots have not always been good at recognising what that heritage is and protecting it when it is threatened. Thus the sellers of these fine examples of the country's vernacular architecture on the north side of Newhaven Main Street got their buyer, and within a few years of this picture being taken in the late nineteenth century, the '60 FEET FRONTAGE' had been demolished and replaced with an unremarkable tenement. It is a story that was repeated across the country on an industrial scale in the late nineteenth and early twentieth centuries as much of the nation's built heritage was reduced to rubble. Often these buildings were in poor shape, and with many being damp and insanitary something had to be done to improve them. Despite this their wholesale demolition is a huge loss. Given the zeal with which this was undertaken, the remarkable thing about Newhaven is not how much was lost, but how much actually survived into a more enlightened age. Now the tenements that replaced these old structures have themselves given way to more modern housing that in appearance harks back to the old vernacular style.

Many of the structures in Newhaven Main Street are modern, but because an effort has been made to reflect the architecture of the old village its character has not been entirely lost. The slightly curved street line remains and is linked to Pier Place and the harbour by closes, lanes and pends. The Marine Hotel occupied the distinctive building at the western end of Pier Place and Main Street, and as befits a hostelry sited next to a busy fishing harbour it made a point of offering its customers 'fish dinners'. This harbourside catering tradition was given a boost in 1993 when Harry Ramsden's restaurant and takeaway was opened in the old fish market sheds, although sadly it has since closed. The market, built in 1896, can be seen to the left of the prominent 'Fishermen's Church' in Pier Place. It was built for a Free Church congregation in 1852 and the steeple was added thirty years later. After successive amalgamations of the Protestant churches it became known as St Andrew's Parish Church of Newhaven in 1929, and stopped being used as a place of worship in 1974. People can now practice their climbing skills in the building, no doubt praying they don't fall off.

In its heyday practically everyone in Newhaven was associated with the fishing industry. Numerous small open boats, like those seen in this picture from *c.*1910 and in the photograph on the front cover, were either based in the harbour or came in to land their catch at the fish market. Herring was the principal target, but the shoals could be unpredictable and Newhaven's boats had none of today's sophisticated devices for locating their often elusive quarry. Nor could they venture far into open waters, so as the herring dwindled the fishing fleet did too. With the demise of the boats, the market ceased to be the bustling place it once was, although one end of the sheds is still used early in the morning to buy and sell fish. The market is now a listed structure and houses an excellent museum which tells the story of the village and its industry. Today the view across to Fife is obscured by modern structures which have been built on the Western Harbour breakwater which butts up to the old harbour wall. The iron lighthouse, on the left, superseded the little stone domed structure in the mid-nineteenth century when the harbour was extended.

In some ways Newhaven harbour was a curious affair which started as a slipway and breakwater and was extended to create a proper harbour. The entrance faced west into the prevailing wind which made it tricky to get in and out of, and even when boats had made harbour the wind funnelling in and swirling round could make it a less than peaceful haven. It was also tidally restricted and prone to silting up, so it required periodic dredging. The market was not Newhaven's only sales outlet for herring. Women of all ages strapped fish-filled creels to their backs and travelled the country selling the contents. The distinctive clothes and street cries of these Newhaven fishwives became familiar wherever they went. Their songs were also made famous by groups wearing traditional dress like the Newhaven Fisherwomen's Choir. This was formed in 1927 as the Newhaven Liberal Club Choir to support the local parliamentary candidate, remaining in existence for just over fifty years, although the perhaps more famous Fisherlassies Choir predated it and outlasted it.

'The camera never lies' is only half of the original saying which concludes 'but liars take photographs': not that this view of Stanley Road tells lies, it's just that the photographer has used a very wide-angle lens, exaggerating the scene. Taken from the building on the corner of Craighall and East Trinity Roads, the picture shows the road as an expansive boulevard instead of an average-sized street. By emphasising its west end it also masks the subtle change in character from the private villas set in their own garden grounds in the foreground, to the less secluded semi-detached houses to the east. Some of the villas have now been flatted or even form the core of small blocks of flats. The wide-angle lens has also made the trams in the picture look like miniatures, but they were not so small and in order to cope with the sharp corners at both the Craighall and Newhaven Road ends, the tracks were reduced to single line curves. Stanley Road was also used as a terminus and could get quite congested, so latterly tram routes terminated the foot of Craighall Road instead.